ECPE MICHIGAN PROFICIENCY LISTENING AND SPEAKING TEST BOOK STUDY GUIDE WITH MP3s AND PRACTICE EXAM QUESTIONS

The Examination for the Certificate of Proficiency in English and ECPE are trademarks of the University of Michigan, in conjunction with Cambridge Assessment English, which are neither affiliated with nor endorse this publication.

ECPE Michigan Proficiency Listening and Speaking Test Book: Study Guide with mp3s and Practice Exam Questions

© COPYRIGHT 1995, 2019 Academic Success Group dba www.michigan-test.com

All rights reserved. No part of this publication may be reproduced, stored in a retrieval system, or transmitted, in any form or by any means, electronic, mechanical, photocopying, recording, or otherwise, without the prior written permission of the copyright owner.

ISBN-13: 978-1-949282-48-1

NOTE: The Examination for the Certificate of Proficiency in English and ECPE are trademarks of the University of Michigan, in conjunction with Cambridge Assessment English, which are neither affiliated with nor endorse this publication.

COPYRIGHT NOTICE TO EDUCATORS

Please respect copyright law. Under no circumstances may you make copies of these materials for distribution to or use by students. Should you wish to use the materials with students, you are required to purchase a copy of this publication for each of your students.

TABLE OF CONTENTS

ECPE LISTENING PRACTICE

ECPE listening test format	1
How to use this publication	2
Sound file access	4

Unit 1
Respond to the recorded questions	5
Short radio report on sports	7

Unit 2
Short conversations	8
Short radio report on broadcasting	10

Unit 3
Respond to the recorded questions	11
Short radio report on education	13

Unit 4
Short conversations	14
Short radio report on national history	16

Unit 5
Respond to the recorded questions	17
Short radio report on dramatic arts	19

Unit 6

    Short conversations   20

    Short radio report on music   22

Unit 7

    Respond to the recorded questions   23

    Short radio report on politics   25

Unit 8

    Short conversations   26

    Short radio report on philosophy   28

Unit 9

    Respond to the recorded questions   29

    Short radio report on farming   31

Unit 10

    Short conversations   32

    Short radio report on dangers to health   34

Unit 11

    Respond to the recorded questions   35

    Short radio report on psychology   37

Unit 12

    Short conversations   38

    Short radio report on exploration   40

Unit 13

    Longer conversations   41

Unit 14

    Longer conversations   43

Unit 15

    Longer radio report on nutrition   45

Unit 16

    Longer radio report on medical topic   46

Unit 17

    Longer radio report on teaching   47

Unit 18

    Longer radio report on smoking   48

ECPE SPEAKING PRACTICE TESTS

ECPE speaking test information   49

ECPE speaking practice test 1   50

ECPE speaking practice test 2   52

ECPE speaking practice test 3   54

ECPE speaking practice test 4   56

ECPE speaking practice test 5   58

Listening Scripts   60

Answer Key   104

ECPE LISTENING TEST FORMAT

The ECPE listening test consists of three parts.

Part 1

In part 1 of the listening test, you will hear 15 short recorded conversations. On your test paper, you will see three printed sentences. You need to select the sentence that is true according to the conversation. Some of the conversations will be very brief, and others will be a bit longer.

Part 2

There are 20 recorded questions on this part of the test. You will listen to each question, and then you will have to select the correct response to each one based on the three answer choices provided.

Part 3

In this part of the listening exam, you will listen to three reports like you will hear on the radio. The reports will normally have more than one person speaking about the topic. There will be three recorded reports and five listening comprehension questions on each report. These recorded reports usually last for three to four minutes each.

Note:

You will have to record your answers on a separate answer sheet. You will hear each part on the listening test only once. The listening test lasts for approximately 30 minutes.

HOW TO USE THIS PUBLICATION

This book is designed to build students' skills for the listening section of the Examination for the Certificate of Proficiency in English. As such, the units are placed into order of difficulty, with the less difficult questions first and the advanced questions at the end of the listening section of the book.

Units 1, 3, 5, 7, 9, and 11

In the first part of each of these units, you will hear recorded questions like those on part 2 of the exam.

Units 2, 4, 6, 8, and 12

Each of these units contains short conversations like you will hear in part 1 of the exam.

Units 1 to 12

In the second half of each unit, you will hear a short radio report with one speaker. These exercises will help prepare you for the radio reports on part 3 of the real exam that have more than one speaker. There are 5 questions after each recording.

Units 13 and 14

These units have longer conversations like you will hear on part 1 of the test.

Units 15 to 18

Each of these recordings contain longer radio reports with more than one speaker, like you will hear on part 3 of the real test. There are 5 questions after each recording.

Idioms on the Exam

Idiomatic language and colloquialisms are very commonly tested on the ECPE listening test.

In order to learn the idioms that are assessed on the ECPE listening exam, this book should be used with our other publication, which is entitled:

Michigan Test Vocabulary Practice with Exercises and Answers: Review of the Vocabulary, Phrasal Verbs, and Idioms on the Michigan English Proficiency Exams (2nd edition)

SOUND FILE ACCESS

To access the recordings, please go to the following webpage:

https://ecpemp3.michigan-test.com

There are links on the above webpage to each of the units in this publication.

For ease of use, the webpage lists the sound files in numerical order by unit number.

UNIT 1

Instructions: For questions 1 to 10 choose the best answers to the questions you hear.

1)   a. I'll finally manage.
        b. No, I'll take my chances.
        c. Yes, it will.

2)   a. I'll say!
        b. Not if I can help it!
        c. Don't you know them?

3)   a. If it comes up.
        b. She will too.
        c. You can count on it.

4)   a. Oh no, not again!
        b. She was at her mother's house.
        c. Yes, I hear it.

5)   a. Yes, a good many.
        b. No, I couldn't picture it.
        c. No, I took them.

6)   a. Yes, his clothes are very nice.
        b. Yes, he's very bright.
        c. No, he wasn't.

7)   a. No problem.
        b. I wouldn't drop it.
        c. I can if you like.

8) a. Yes, I promise to write.
   b. No, I wouldn't.
   c. Yes, I'm touchy.

9) a. No, he was picked.
   b. Yes, he was fighting.
   c. Yes, he was asking for it.

10) a. Never enough money.
    b. Not much.
    c. Let's wait and see.

EXERCISE 1

Instructions: Now you will hear a brief segment from a radio program. As you listen, you may take notes. Then you will answer some questions about it.

1) When did the first official Olympic Games take place?
   a. 393 AD
   b. 776 BC
   c. 1896 AD

2) How many events did the Pentathlon include?
   a. 3
   b. 5
   c. 7

3) Who was not allowed to compete in the ancient Olympic Games?
   a. Chariot racers
   b. Greek-born men
   c. Women

4) What is the IOC?
   a. International Olympic Committee
   b. International Official City
   c. International Olympic City

5) What happens during the parade of nations?
   a. The athletes take the Olympic Oath.
   b. The athletes compete in their first event.
   c. The athletes march around the stadium.

UNIT 2

Instructions: For questions 1 to 10 choose the best explanation for what the speakers have said.

1)   a. He's telling her not to discourage him.
         b. He definitely won't be admitted.
         c. He has changed the subject to the weather.

2)   a. They have a mutual friend named Frank.
         b. He wants to speak honestly.
         c. He really likes Martha.

3)   a. He will send a letter to John.
         b. He has received a letter from John.
         c. He will tell her when he has heard.

4)   a. His new apartment is larger that his previous one.
         b. He is getting used to it.
         c. He doesn't like his new place at all.

5)   a. She is angry at him.
         b. He thought they were going to a restaurant.
         c. He thinks she's unappreciative.

6)   a. He doesn't like Disneyland.
         b. He thinks she's crazy.
         c. He thinks she's made an unusual suggestion.

7)   a. He is very angry with his mother.
         b. He lives next door to his mother.
         c. He is worried about his mother.

8) a. He wants her to explain it.
   b. He wants her to turn on the lamp.
   c. He wants to see her homework.

9) a. She wishes that his sister were dead.
   b. He is fed up with this topic.
   c. His sister annoys both of them.

10) a. He doesn't have any money.
    b. He has lost his billfold.
    c. He had to pay for a problem with his car.

EXERCISE 2

Instructions: Now you will hear a brief segment from a radio program. As you listen, you may take notes. Then you will answer some questions about it.

1) Where is it usually best to begin a career in television?
   a. At the local level
   b. At the national level
   c. At the international level

2) According to the speaker, how is success measured?
   a. By the amount of money made
   b. By obtaining syndication
   c. By the number of viewers

3) What is of utmost importance in order to get a job as a TV celebrity?
   a. What you know
   b. Who you know
   c. How much you know

4) How important is academic training for jobs in journalism or broadcasting?
   a. very important
   b. somewhat important
   c. unimportant

5) For jobs in journalism, how should a person speak?
   a. loudly
   b. quickly
   c. clearly

UNIT 3

Instructions: For questions 1 to 10 choose the best answers to the questions you hear.

1)   a. They will be performing.
        b. No, I'll wait until the end.
        c. Only if it's intermittent.

2)   a. Yes, and it was really awful.
        b. It wasn't accidental.
        c. That would never happen.

3)   a. Yes, more than I expected.
        b. No, he said not to.
        c. Yes, he will.

4)   a. My job isn't easy.
        b. John quit too.
        c. Yes, without a doubt.

5)   a. Yes, I did.
        b. Not that great.
        c. No, it wasn't.

6)   a. I haven't seen her.
        b. Yes, next Tuesday.
        c. Not if I can help it.

7)   a. I don't like it.
        b. No, the other one.
        c. Sorry, I'm using it right now.

8) a. No, I didn't see you.
    b. Yes, I saw him.
    c. No, not yet.

9) a. Much too much.
    b. I'd say one too many.
    c. Yes, many.

10) a. No, she'll be alone.
    b. No, she will come.
    c. Yes, she won't come.

EXERCISE 3

Instructions: Now you will hear a brief segment from a radio program. As you listen, you may take notes. Then you will answer some questions about it.

1) Where is teaching especially challenging?
   a. At elementary schools
   b. At private high schools
   c. At state high schools

2) What poses a serious problem to teachers?
   a. disruptive infants
   b. violent teenagers
   c. inattentive youngsters

3) What might be an outcome of funding problems?
   a. a national economic downturn
   b. state bureaucracy
   c. discontinuing classes or programs

4) Why have some teachers changed careers?
   a. They have become bored with teaching.
   b. They have found their work stressful.
   c. They failed to receive personal financial assistance.

5) What do dedicated teachers find rewarding?
   a. Financial availability
   b. The changing demands of the educational system
   c. Helping students obtain knowledge

UNIT 4

Instructions: For questions 1 to 10 choose the best explanation for what the speakers have said.

1)   a. They both knew it would happen.
        b. Billy took money to buy a cake.
        c. It's really unbelievable.

2)   a. He wants to start in the autumn.
        b. He can't because his grades have declined.
        c. He isn't interested in going to college.

3)   a. Betty has always been overweight.
        b. Betty eats a lot of junk food.
        c. Betty will go on a diet soon.

4)   a. They thought the building was on fire.
        b. The meeting lasted longer than they expected.
        c. They all wanted to have a cigarette.

5)   a. Mary Jo is quite bold.
        b. Mary Jo is nervous.
        c. Mary Jo is worried.

6)   a. He will definitely get the money.
        b. He wishes he could get the money.
        c. He feels fortunate to have gotten the money.

7)   a. Anna always works hard.
        b. Anna works in a factory right now.
        c. He thinks Anna doesn't work hard enough.

8) a. He has already told the professor.
   b. He will tell the professor.
   c. He won't tell the professor.

9) a. Bob lives near a river.
   b. He is worried about getting across the river.
   c. They will make a decision when necessary to do so.

10) a. It's news to him.
    b. He already knew that John is mean.
    c. They both like John.

EXERCISE 4

Instructions: Now you will hear a brief segment from a radio program. As you listen, you may take notes. Then you will answer some questions about it.

1) When did the first Pilgrims leave England?
   a. 1608
   b. 1617
   c. 1620

2) What prevented the Pilgrims from beginning their journey to America?
   a. lack of education
   b. lack of social status
   c. lack of financing

3) How many days was the *Mayflower* at sea?
   a. 30
   b. 35
   c. 65

4) What town did the Pilgrims establish?
   a. Weston
   b. Plymouth
   c. Boston

5) How did the Pilgrims establish new laws?
   a. by governing the Plymouth Colony
   b. through political advisors
   c. by writing the Mayflower Compact

UNIT 5

Instructions: For questions 1 to 10 choose the best answers for the questions you hear.

1) a. No, I have a bad back.
    b. You bet! Hop in.
    c. Sorry, I'm not that strong.

2) a. No, he'll never agree to that.
    b. Yes, although he doesn't like airplanes.
    c. You know he's afraid of heights.

3) a. Yeah, it was pretty tough but I managed.
    b. Yes, there was parking.
    c. No, not nearly enough.

4) a. I can't. It's already full.
    b. You're welcome.
    c. Only if it's available.

5) a. Yes, before then.
    b. Only once.
    c. No, not just me.

6) a. Yes, I remember.
    b. No, it didn't suit me.
    c. Of course I did.

7) a. Yes, he'll call next week.
    b. No, to touch base.
    c. Yes, he is very demonstrative.

8)   a. Providing it happens.
        b. Where? Here?
        c. Yes, it's to be written down.

9)   a. She won't come.
        b. No, you won't.
        c. Yes, I'm exhausted.

10)   a. No, I didn't want to.
        b. Yes, I wanted to.
        c. Sounds great to me!

EXERCISE 5

Instructions: Now you will hear a brief segment from a radio program. As you listen, you may take notes. Then you will answer some questions about it.

1) What is one good reason to study dramatic arts?
   a. to improve self-confidence
   b. to help employers
   c. to excel at college

2) What are students expected to do when attending performances?
   a. passively observe
   b. practice public speaking
   c. analyze the production

3) What subject are students expected to study?
   a. poetry of the theater
   b. politics of the theater
   c. history of the theater

4) What is stage fright?
   a. fear of dramatic developments
   b. fear of performing
   c. fear of production

5) What do the principles of acting for film not include?
   a. mechanics of film production
   b. emotional responsiveness
   c. understanding particular characters

UNIT 6

Instructions: For questions 1 to 10 choose the best explanation for what the speakers have said.

1)   a. Her husband should mind his own business.
        b. Her husband's actions should show his intentions.
        c. Her husband is a good cook.

2)   a. His son isn't on the team because he didn't play well enough.
        b. His son's grades were too low.
        c. His son is on academic probation.

3)   a. She can make the decision.
        b. He has decided to leave her.
        c. He wants to eat somewhere else.

4)   a. The quiz won't be a surprise.
        b. He wants her to guess.
        c. He doesn't know either.

5)   a. His wife isn't a very good housekeeper.
        b. Al must deal with the consequences of his actions.
        c. They are going to get back together.

6)   a. He couldn't stand it any longer.
        b. He doesn't like working with his hands.
        c. He isn't working anywhere right now.

7)   a. They found a table to sit at.
        b. He thinks that Bob is outstanding.
        c. Bob didn't show up.

8) a. He slept in too late this morning
   b. He doesn't feel like it.
   c. He has been rather sick lately.

9) a. He's telling her to relax.
   b. He's telling her to lose weight.
   c. She really gets him down.

10) a. His wife is pleasant.
    b. He regrets marrying her.
    c. It is difficult to make his wife happy.

EXERCISE 6

Instructions: Now you will hear a brief segment from a radio program. As you listen, you may take notes. Then you will answer some questions about it.

1) What best describes the origins of music?
   a. monophonic
   b. multiphonic
   c. polyphonic

2) What happened as polyphonic music began to develop?
   a. Monophonic music became less popular.
   b. A wider range of voices began to be used.
   c. Several notes were combined in a single series.

3) What happened during the sixteenth century?
   a. Musical instruments were used more and more often.
   b. There were special developments in the opera.
   c. The orchestra began to die out.

4) When was Baroque music developed?
   a. the sixteenth century
   b. the seventeenth century
   c. the eighteenth century

5) What marks the end of the classical period?
   a. the development of the symphony
   b. the study of German composers abroad
   c. the music of Beethoven

UNIT 7

Instructions: For questions 1 to 10 choose the best answers to the questions you hear.

1)   a. No, we're going to stay in motels.
         b. Yes, it will.
         c. No, we will camp.

2)   a. She won't serve.
         b. Can't you see how busy they are?
         c. The food is always good here.

3)   a. Yes, he was clearly at fault.
         b. Yes, it happens.
         c. No, it wouldn't.

4)   a. Yes, whiskey is my preference.
         b. Jack Daniel's is my favorite.
         c. No, I wouldn't say that.

5)   a. Like cats and dogs!
         b. Yes, they got along.
         c. No, they didn't.

6)   a. No number 12.
         b. It isn't on schedule today.
         c. Yes, here you go.

7)   a. Sorry, resting isn't permitted in here.
         b. No, not today.
         c. Yes, down the hall and on the left.

8)   a. Yeah, I'm sure she made the whole thing up.
          b. No, not until Monday.
          c. No, she never did.

9)   a. Yes, he pulls them.
          b. Yes, he's very influential.
          c. No, he pushes it.

10)   a. Yeah, they're like cowboys.
          b. Yeah, they tied me in knots.
          c. Yes, I learned everything I needed to know.

EXERCISE 7

Instructions: Now you will hear a brief segment from a radio program. As you listen, you may take notes. Then you will answer some questions about it.

1) What organization occupied the offices that were burglarized?
   a. the Democracy Nationalism Committee
   b. the Democratic National Committee
   c. the Democratic National Caucus

2) Who initially discovered the burglary?
   a. the ringleader
   b. the police
   c. the security guard

3) What did the burglars have in their pockets?
   a. one-hundred-dollar bills
   b. burglary tools
   c. tape

4) What did the police investigation confirm?
   a. The burglars were part of a professional ring.
   b. Several items were stolen.
   c. The burglars had removed telephone equipment.

5) What is CREEP?
   a. Committee for Reconciliation of the Presidency
   b. Committee for the Re-election of the President
   c. Committee for the Resurgence of the Presidency

UNIT 8

Instructions: For questions 1 to 10 choose the best explanation for what the speakers have said.

1)   a. He will go.
       b. He won't go.
       c. He wants to see how much it costs.

2)   a. He thinks Bob is hilarious.
       b. He doesn't think Bob is amusing.
       c. He thinks Bob is totally crazy.

3)   a. Mary's dad is happy-go-lucky.
       b. Mary's dad is a disciplinarian.
       c. Mary's dad is away from home.

4)   a. He wants to know when it happened.
       b. He wants to know where it happened.
       c. He wants to know why it happened.

5)   a. He thinks that there is no difference between the two crimes.
       b. He wants to know the amount of their loss.
       c. He wonders if the same things were stolen.

6)   a. He was removed from the exam.
       b. He figures: "That's life!"
       c. He feels crushed.

7)   a. Bob is incompetent.
       b. Bob knows what he is doing.
       c. Bob's success was accidental.

8) a. Things aren't going too well.
   b. He is angry with her for asking about it.
   c. He can't to talk right now.

9) a. They will decide at the corner.
   b. He was driving too fast.
   c. He didn't understand the directions either.

10) a. He has no interest in the subject.
    b. He disagrees with her.
    c. He agrees with her.

EXERCISE 8

Instructions: Now you will hear a brief segment from a radio program. As you listen, you may take notes. Then you will answer some questions about it.

1) Which question is central to the investigation of human choice?
   a. Do human being have control over their futures?
   b. Are human beings capable of making good decisions?
   c. Why do human beings have to choose?

2) What is epistemology?
   a. the study of being
   b. the study of knowledge
   c. the study of decision making

3) What aspects of human personality are investigated?
   a. emotional
   b. spiritual
   c. both b and c

4) What is the fourth problem area of the philosophy of human nature?
   a. unity
   b. complexity
   c. personality

5) The course studies the writings of which philosopher?
   a. Platinus
   b. Plato
   c. Phaedrus

UNIT 9

Instructions: For questions 1 to 10 choose the best answers to the questions you hear.

1)
   a. No, I'm trying to quit.
   b. I couldn't. There was a yellow line.
   c. Yes, it is prohibited.

2)
   a. It will happen tomorrow.
   b. No special oysters.
   c. Yes, but unfortunately they are sold out today.

3)
   a. Okay, so I lied!
   b. No " if's," "and's," or "but's"!
   c. Yes, I will smoke.

4)
   a. No, it's by the sink.
   b. Yes, but be gentle.
   c. No, for washing.

5)
   a. Well, it depends.
   b. Of course not! I don't have any kids!
   c. Yeah, like a baby.

6)
   a. Yes, it helps the situation.
   b. Yeah, it really gets me down.
   c. No, many people are.

7)
   a. No, she's not home right now.
   b. Yes, she's controlling.
   c. Yes, I feel really comfortable there.

8)   a. Yes, everyone was in favor of it.
         b. No, it was my favorite.
         c. Yes, I voted.

9)   a. Yes, dial it.
         b. Yes, add a little water.
         c. No, make orange juice.

10)   a. No, totally private.
         b. Yes, everyone was outraged.
         c. Yes, it was decreasing.

EXERCISE 9

Instructions: Now you will hear a brief segment from a radio program. As you listen, you may take notes. Then you will answer some questions about it.

1) What have American farmers realized about organic farming?
   a. It is more costly than conventional farming.
   b. It is more cost-effective than conventional farming.
   c. It results in lower profits than conventional farming.

2) In what way does organic farming benefit the environment?
   a. It does not use chemicals.
   b. It uses only synthetic materials.
   c. It can be used to control produce.

3) What comment did the speaker make about the certification process?
   a. Most farmers can pass it easily.
   b. It uses a great deal of processing.
   c. It involves quite strict standards.

4) Which concern do some people have about organic food?
   a. cost
   b. safety
   c. production methods

5) How does organic farming improve wildlife?
   a. It results in a greater variety of species.
   b. It reduces the number of insects.
   c. It increases livestock.

UNIT 10

Instructions: For questions 1 to 10 choose the best explanation for what the speakers have said.

1)   a. He wonders if she has really looked everywhere.
         b. He has a low opinion of her.
         c. He will help her look now.

2)   a. She is a creep.
         b. He was really frightened.
         c. He was only creeping along.

3)   a. They can't stand Jason.
         b. Jason is very voluble.
         c. Jason is rather reticent.

4)   a. Tom has a job in finance and investments.
         b. Tom is flat broke.
         c. Tom is not very smart.

5)   a. He has a sweet tooth.
         b. The exam was quite tough.
         c. The exam was very easy.

6)   a. Sue doesn't drink coffee.
         b. Johns needs to face reality.
         c. They will reconcile.

7)   a. He goes only when the moon is full.
         b. He goes frequently.
         c. He seldom goes.

8) a. She did the worst thing imaginable.
   b. She is always lying.
   c. She was confronted with a dilemma.

9) a. He's not happy about going home.
   b. It's a sticky situation.
   c. It is very late.

10) a. She shouldn't slander other people.
    b. She is quite a shifty character.
    c. Annette's reputation is untarnished.

EXERCISE 10

Instructions: Now you will hear a brief segment from a radio program. As you listen, you may take notes. Then you will answer some questions about it.

1) What usually happens when cells divide?
   a. the abnormal growth of organs
   b. tumors begin to grow
   c. the human body is kept healthy

2) What is metastasis?
   a. the growth of cancer in a cell
   b. the growth of cancer inside a tumor
   c. the spread of cancer from a tumor

3) What is the biggest cause of cancer in America?
   a. poor nutrition
   b. overexposure to the sun
   c. smoking

4) How does cancer compare to other diseases?
   a. It is the first leading cause of death.
   b. It is the second leading cause of death.
   c. It is the third leading cause of death.

5) How many American women will eventually develop cancer?
   a. one-fourth
   b. one-third
   c. one-half

UNIT 11

Instructions: For questions 1 to 10 choose the best answers to the questions you hear.

1)   a. I'd be glad to.
        b. Get away from here.
        c. Yes, I'll take off.

2)   a. You don't say!
        b. Yes, he said so.
        c. I'll get the loan after all.

3)   a. No, I don't hear very well.
        b. What a shame!
        c. Yes, it's burning.

4)   a. Yes, I had to apply myself.
        b. Yes, I did.
        c. Yes, I wanted it.

5)   a. No, I wouldn't hide anything from you.
        b. Yes, nothing.
        c. No, it's down there.

6)   a. Yes, I earn one.
        b. $5,000 a month.
        c. I'm a lawyer.

7)   a. I really doubt it.
        b. She leaves on Thursday.
        c. She'll stay until Friday.

8) a. Yes, it's as good as new.
   b. Yes, for good.
   c. No, for bad.

9) a. No, he's all but incompetent.
   b. No, he's at his desk.
   c. Yes, he's at work today.

10) a. No, thanks. I'm full.
    b. Yes, I could use some assistance.
    c. No help, please.

EXERCISE 11

Instructions: Now you will hear a brief segment from a radio program. As you listen, you may take notes. Then you will answer some questions about it.

1) How many personality types are there?
   a. two
   b. four
   c. sixteen

2) What does the term "extrovert" mean?
   a. preferring to interact with others
   b. preferring to keep to oneself
   c. preferring to make decisions externally

3) What does the second category include?
   a. the individual's relationships with others
   b. the individual's method of receiving information
   c. the individual's method of making decisions

4) What function involves reliance upon facts?
   a. thinking
   b. feeling
   c. sensing

5) What function is the opposite of judging?
   a. intuiting
   b. perceiving
   c. internalizing

UNIT 12

Instructions: For questions 1 to 10 choose the best explanation for what the speakers have said.

1) a. They enjoy mountain climbing.
    b. He made her hitch-hike.
    c. He told Sue to hit the road.

2) a. He said it's impossible.
    b. He questioned her.
    c. He doubts her.

3) a. They both want to find a solution.
    b. Everyone knows he has a heart problem.
    c. He feels disconcerted about her suggestion.

4) a. Good performance on the final is crucial.
    b. His performance was indifferent.
    c. He is making a dare.

5) a. They are talking about baseball.
    b. They have agreed to keep in contact.
    c. He feels upset.

6) a. He thinks Bob is a flirt.
    b. He is envious of Bob's wife.
    c. He thinks Bob is playing with fire.

7) a. He has had the same hairstyle for ages.
    b. He doesn't want to see Sharon.
    c. He just wants to be himself.

8) a. He has made his wishes known indirectly.
    b. He blurted it out.
    c. He is feeling ambivalent.

9) a. He's always been a dreamer.
    b. He had a wild time.
    c. It was even better than he had imagined.

10) a. She is nit-picking.
    b. Her boss is witty.
    c. She should not have jeopardized her well-being.

EXERCISE 12

Now you will hear a brief segment from a radio program. As you listen, you may take notes. Then you will answer some questions about it.

1) How did Lewis and Clark become friends?
   a. They were neighbors.
   b. They worked in the same branch of the government.
   c. They were in the same local division of the army.

2) Who offered Lewis the job of exploring the west?
   a. Jefferson
   b. Clark
   c. Congress

3) Why did Clark travel with Lewis?
   a. Lewis felt he needed a partner.
   b. Clark felt he needed a partner.
   c. Because of financial restrictions.

4) Why were Lewis and Clark good as partners?
   a. They each had different personal characteristics.
   b. They were dissimilar in temperament.
   c. They shared many traits and abilities.

5) What happened after the expedition had finished?
   a. Clark died unexpectedly.
   b. The Louisiana Territory was purchased.
   c. The Missouri River was discovered.

UNIT 13

Instructions: Choose the statement that is true according to each conversation that you hear.

1) A. He is looking forward to getting a scholarship
   B. He thinks he will be lucky.
   C. He thinks he probably won't get a scholarship.

2) A. The man is fed up with her.
   B. The man is excited.
   C. The man is resigned.

3) A. The man feels enthusiastic.
   B. The man is unhappy about his new job.
   C. The man has had an argument with his boss.

4) A. The woman suggests that the man be more patient.
   B. The man's wife has misled him.
   C. The woman suggests that the man and his wife go on a trip.

5) A. The man will speak to the coach.
   B. The man will speak to his son.
   C. The man won't take the woman's advice.

6) A. The woman wants to talk before seeing each other on Saturday.
   B. The woman will be with other friends go out on Saturday.
   C. The man will call the woman later that day.

7) A. She has given some good advice.
   B. He thinks she's trying to make him disheartened.
   C. She doesn't want to attend the parade.

8) A. Mary is not being responsible about her job.
   B. Mary is nervous about her work situation.
   C. Mary is speaking badly about other people.

9) A. The speakers' friend is overweight.
   B. The speakers' friend has diabetes.
   C. The speakers' friend eats junk food occasionally.

10) A. He detests these events.
    B. He really enjoys classical music.
    C. He is starting to like concerts a bit more.

11) A. The man wants to find a new bank.
    B. The man wants to wait to see what happens.
    C. The man wants to think about other options.

12) A. The manager apologized to the man and the woman.
    B. The employees saw the manager standing somewhere else.
    C. The manager didn't come to the appointment.

13) A. The speakers' classmate bought a video game.
    B. The speakers' classmate was in jail for stealing.
    C. The speakers' classmate was in bed ill.

14) A. Their relationship is jovial.
    B. Their relationship is acrimonious.
    C. Their relationship is friendly.

15) A. The woman thought the man should be more grateful.
    B. The woman knew the work was challenging.
    C. The woman is pleasantly surprised.

UNIT 14

Instructions: Choose the statement that is true according to each conversation that you hear.

1) A. The woman had a disagreement with the man.
   B. The woman had a disagreement with her friend.
   C. The woman didn't want to hurt her friend's feelings.

2) A. The man going to take a trip.
   B. The man is going to speak to his teacher.
   C. The man going to study.

3) A. The woman needs to stop gossiping.
   B. The woman needs to apologize to her husband.
   C. The woman needs to stop complaining.

4) A. They couldn't understand the professor.
   B. The professor changed the date of the essay.
   C. The professor was ill.

5) A. The man didn't feel afraid at the movie.
   B. The man doesn't really like scary movies.
   C. The hadn't been to a movie like this for a while.

6) A. Toby will get his job back.
   B. Toby likes to drink coffee.
   C. Toby is unaware that his situation is serious.

7) A. The woman doesn't have children of her own yet.
   B. The woman lets her children decide things.
   C. The woman will persuade Amal to come to the party.

8) A. The man is flustered.
   B. The man has accepted the situation.
   C. The man is bored.

9) A. Carlos can give business advice.
   B. Carlos can give relationship advice.
   C. Carlos can go to the interview.

10) A. The man will go on a hike with his friend.
    B. The man doesn't want to change.
    C. The man will get more comfortable.

11) A. The speakers will go out immediately.
    B. The speakers will eat their meal next.
    C. The speakers will do their homework next.

12) A. The man has lost the woman's jacket.
    B. The woman thinks the man questions her too much.
    C. The woman doesn't like the jacket.

13) A. He doesn't want to speak about the exam.
    B. He thought the exam was only a bit difficult.
    C. He is worried that he failed.

14) A. Their friend's dress was beautiful.
    B. Their friend was going to return a worn dress.
    C. Their friend's cake was delicious.

15) A. The woman wants to lessen the consequences.
    B. The employee is late to work.
    C. The employee is leaving his job.

UNIT 15

Instructions: Now you will hear a brief segment from a radio program. As you listen, you may take notes. Then you will answer some questions about it.

1) What is the main idea of the report?
   A. The impact of nutrition on health
   B. The dangers of excessive dieting
   C. New advice about protein consumption

2) What is stated about fruit and vegetables?
   A. Each person should consume an apple daily.
   B. It is important to eat at least five portions daily.
   C. Medical practitioners give different advice about fruit and vegetables.

3) What is mentioned about protein consumption?
   A. A person should be careful to eat enough dairy products.
   B. Red meat should be eaten instead of rich cheese.
   C. Every person should monitor their intake of fatty protein.

4) How does the speaker support the comment about food additives?
   A. By giving reasons for their dangers
   B. By describing the public's general preference
   C. By discussing a specific medical case study

5) Which one of the following statements is correct according to the report?
   A. Healthy nutrition means that food is consumed from five major groups.
   B. Sugar consumption need not be restricted.
   C. Processed and convenience foods may damage the health.

UNIT 16

Instructions: Now you will hear a brief segment from a radio program. As you listen, you may take notes. Then you will answer some questions about it.

1) What is the main idea of this discussion?
   A. the function of the human brain and how to measure it
   B. the discovery of brain waves
   C. the reasons for brain dysfunction

2) What was Edgar Adrian's most important discovery?
   A. The brain emits electrical impulses.
   B. The heart has electrical activity.
   C. The brain and the heart are similar physiologically.

3) Why is the definition of brain death controversial?
   A. Because the purpose of the cerebral cortex is unknown.
   B. Because other parts of the body may function after a person is no longer capable of rational thought.
   C. Because of legal regulations.

4) From the report, what can be inferred about PET scans?
   A. They are more or less identical to the CAT scan.
   B. Patients would probably rather forego PET scans.
   C. They are superior to the MRI scan.

5) How does the speaker support his comments about the indispensability of the MRI scan?
   A. By citing a medical authority
   B. By giving statistical data
   C. By providing a reason

UNIT 17

Instructions: Now you will hear a brief segment from a radio program. As you listen, you may take notes. Then you will answer some questions about it.

1) What is the main idea of the report?
   A. Different types of educational strategies
   B. The variety of assessment models available to teachers
   C. The specific aspects of the student readiness model

2) How does the speaker support his statement that "student readiness is not a static entity"?
   A. By mentioning that some students have a "comfort zone"
   B. By discussing the needs of above-average students
   C. By explaining the ways in which a student's level can change

3) What does the man state about curriculum design?
   A. It is the duty of the teachers to decide which design is best.
   B. Teachers usually disagree about the curriculum.
   C. Question adjustment often thwarts curriculum design.

4) Which one of the following is the best description of the "question adjustment" strategy?
   A. The teacher's questions should exceed the students' level in order to challenge all of the students.
   B. The teacher should ask questions at various levels of difficulty.
   C. The teacher should ask mainly easy questions to build student confidence.

5) Which one of the following statements is correct according to the report?
   A. Formal assessments determine a student's grade for a course.
   B. Students prefer informal assessment.
   C. Students are confident when they have low readiness.

UNIT 18

Instructions: Now you will hear a brief segment from a radio program. As you listen, you may take notes. Then you will answer some questions about it.

1) What is the main idea of the discussion?
   A. reasons for the decrease in teenage smoking
   B. recent trends in teenage smoking
   C. reasons for teenage experimental smoking

2) Besides peer pressure, what reason is given for the increase in teenage smoking?
   A. the decrease in the price of cigarettes
   B. feelings of alienation from within the family
   C. lawsuits against tobacco companies

3) From the report, what can be inferred about lawsuits against tobacco companies?
   A. They affected affluent families more than poor families.
   B. They affected teenagers more than adults.
   C. Cigarette companies had to reduce their prices to increase demand.

4) What is the outcome of teenage experimental smoking?
   A. Most experimental smokers do not manage to quit.
   B. It causes an increase in cigarette prices.
   C. It can lead to drug addiction.

5) How does the speaker support his comments about experimental smoking?
   A. By giving an example
   B. By giving statistical data
   C. By citing a medical authority

ECPE SPEAKING TEST

Format of the ECPE Speaking Exam

You will take your ECPE speaking exam with another student. Two examiners will listen to your conversation and evaluate your speaking skills.

Students will be given cards that contain different information.

You will need to share your information with the other student and listen to the options that he or she presents to you.

The examiners will give scores from 1 to 5 in each of these three areas:

(1) interaction ability, (2) language skills, and (3) fluency and understandability.

Stages of the Speaking Response:

The examiners look for five different stages in your spoken response:

Stage 1 – You need to introduce and summarize your topic.

Stage 2 – You will explain the different choices to the other student and recommend the option that you think is best.

Stage 3 – You will need to listen to the other student, and then agree or disagree with him or her on the points he or she puts forward.

Stage 4 – You need to present your options clearly and try to persuade the other student that your choice is the best.

Stage 5 – You have to support and defend your opinion when trying to reach a final consensus.

Your final speaking score will be converted to a scale of 0 to 1000.

ECPE SPEAKING PRACTICE TESTS

Speaking Practice Test 1

The two of you are on a selection committee that is going to choose a student for a $500 college scholarship.

Four different students have been selected, and you each will be provided with a description of two of them. However, you can choose only one student to receive the scholarship.

You will need to describe the students on your lists so that the two of you can select the one that you both agree is the best.

Student 1

SALLY SMITH
- Single mother
- In trouble as teenager
- Obtained high school diploma at age 28
- High entrance exam score
- Above average intelligence
- Working as volunteer for local Red Cross

DARNELL JACKSON
- From disadvantaged background
- Low-income level
- Attended college previously but quit
- Now extremely motivated
- Will work part-time while studying
- Lives in another state

Student 2

FATIMA ABDULLAH
- Bullied in high school
- Graduated top of class
- Highest entrance exam score in history
- Extremely intelligent
- Volunteer for disadvantaged children's group
- From wealthy background

HARUTO SUZUKI
- International student
- Studying to become doctor
- High grades in science subjects
- Excellent score on English proficiency test
- Does not interact well with others
- Will use money for his flight to college

Speaking Practice Test 2

You have been given $100 and will donate $20 to five different charitable causes. Charitable causes have been selected from four different groups, with various recipients in each group. However, you can choose only one group for your donations.

You will be given descriptions of the recipients for two of the groups.

You will need to describe the items on your lists so that the two of you can choose the donation for the group that you both agree is the most important.

Student 1

COMMUNITY ASSISTANCE
- Blind and visually-impaired children
- Deaf and hard-of-hearing people
- Neglected animals
- Nursing homes for the elderly
- Homeless and vulnerable people

EDUCATIONAL ORGANIZATIONS
- Programs for children with special needs
- College scholarships for low-income students
- Library for elementary school
- Computers for middle school
- Instruments for high-school band

Student 2

AID FOR VETERANS

- Veterans' mental health program
- Hospital care for veterans
- Veterans' social and entertainment programs
- Commemorative garden in local park
- Assistance to soldiers returning from military service

ARTS AND LOCAL HISTORY
- Modern art gallery
- Local orchestras and choirs
- Decorative statue for town square
- Repair of historical buildings
- Webpage management for local history website

Speaking Practice Test 3

The two of you are students in a class that is going on a weekend trip.

Four different types of trips have been selected, and you each will be provided with a description of two of them.

You have to select a trip for your entire class.

You will need to describe the trips on your lists so that the two of you can choose the one that you both agree is the best.

Student 1

BEACH VACATION
- Accommodation in beach huts
- No electricity
- Portable toilets on site
- No shower facilities available
- Students bring own food
- Cost: $10 per student

LUXURY HOTEL AND SPA
- Hotel complex one hour north of town
- Transportation to hotel provided
- One treatment in the spa included
- Two students per room
- Meals in hotel restaurant at own expense
- Cost: $45 per student

Student 2

TRIP TO CHICAGO, ILLINOIS
- Tour of historic buildings
- Boat trip on lake
- Lunch each day included
- Flight included
- Students find own accommodation
- Cost: $50 per student

CAMPING VACATION
- State park with scenic views
- Tents and supplies provided
- Four students in each tent
- Toilets and showers in building on grounds
- Basic meals cooked on open fire
- Cost: $5 per student

Speaking Practice Test 4

The two of you have won a competition. You will need to decide which prizes to accept for a new apartment that the two of you will share.

Items have been selected for four different rooms of the apartment. However, you can choose your prize for only one room.

You will be given descriptions of the items for two of the rooms.

You will need to describe the items so that the two of you can choose the prize for the room that you both agree is the most important.

Student 1

KITCHEN:
- High-powered microwave
- Set of decorative ceramic plates
- Set of matching coffee mugs
- Set of silverware
- High-capacity washing machine
- Energy-efficient clothes dryer

DINING ROOM:
- Large wooden table
- 4 wooden chairs
- Small lamp with shade
- Large rug
- Vacuum cleaner with attachments
- Decorative vase

Student 2

LIVING ROOM:
- Digital music center with blue-tooth
- Smart TV with wi-fi connectivity
- One-month subscription to Netflix
- Decorative cushions
- Candles in various scents
- Curtains or other window coverings

BATHROOM:
- Shower curtain
- Plush bath mat
- Electric wall-mounted towel warmer
- Jacuzzi attachment for bathtub
- Cosmetics organizer
- Small cupboard with three shelves

Speaking Practice Test 5

The two of you are on a medical committee that is going to choose an uninsured patient for hospital treatment at no cost.

Four different patients have been selected, and you each will be provided with a description of two of them. However, you can select only one patient to receive treatment.

You will need to describe the patients on your lists so that the two of you can choose the one that you both agree is the best.

Student 1

NEIL LOCKSLEY
- Suffers from heart disease
- Needs heart transplant
- Requires 20 days in hospital
- Has 6 children and 15 grandchildren
- Smokes ten cigarettes per day
- Aged 58

MARIA LOPEZ
- Has blood disorder
- Requires daily transfusions
- Needs special machine for treatment
- Machine can also be used by similar patients
- Machine same cost as two years in hospital
- Aged 32

Student 2

BORAK SLOVINSKI
- Suffers from cancer
- Illness is incurable
- In great deal of pain
- Needs palliative hospital care
- Life expectancy is 2 months
- Aged 78

SHANIKA PATMORE
- Premature as baby
- Suffers from cerebral palsy
- Needs therapy to learn to walk
- Duration of therapy: 18 months
- No overnight hospital stays required
- Aged 2 years

LISTENING SCRIPTS

Unit 1

1) Aren't you going to study for your final tomorrow?

2) Don't he and his twin brother bear a striking resemblance to one another?

3) Will you perform in the upcoming concert?

4) Did you hear that Sarah has been admitted to the hospital again?

5) Did you take a lot of pictures on vacation?

6) Isn't Johnny a smart little boy?

7) Do you mind if I drop in sometime?

8) Will you keep in touch?

9) Did he want to pick a fight?

10) How much money do you have?

Exercise 1

The Olympic Games have a long and rich history. The first official Olympic Games took place in Athens in 1896, although experts point out that there is evidence of ancient Olympic Games taking place as early as 776 BC. Athletes in these ancient games competed on the plains of the Greek city of Olympia. The ancient Olympic Games were part of a religious festival and continued for nearly twelve centuries, until banned by Byzantine Emperor Theodosius in 393 AD.

The ancient Olympic Games consisted of several athletic events. Perhaps the most grueling sport was the Pentathlon, an event which included five parts: running, jumping, wrestling, boxing, and the discus throw. The ancient games also included equestrian events, such as horse and chariot racing.

While women were forbidden to compete or even to enter the stadium during the ancient games, many female athletes compete in various events in today's Olympic Games. In addition, although only Greek-born men were allowed to compete in the ancient games, men and women from all over the world come to compete and represent their countries in the modern Olympic Games.

Nowadays, the Olympic Games are governed and organized on an international level by the International Olympic Committee, known as the IOC. The IOC establishes the program of events and chooses the city in which the games are to be held. On the national level, each country that sends athletes to the games has a National Olympic Committee that oversees the participation of the athletes for their countries.

The opening ceremony of the games is held in a stadium in a major city. After the parade of nations, in which the athletes march around the stadium to represent their host country, the athletes take the Olympic Oath. The games, which are said to promote friendship and understanding among nations, then officially begin.

Unit 2

1) - Your chances of getting into law school are slim.

- Well, don't rain on my parade!

2) - What's your opinion of Martha?

- Can I be frank?

3) - Any news from John?

- Not yet, but I'll keep you posted.

4) - How are you liking your new apartment?

- It's starting to grow on me.

5) - Haven't you made supper yet?

- You really take me for granted!

6) - Let's go to Disneyland for vacation.

- Wow! What's come over you?

7) - Any word from your mother?

- No, and I'm just beside myself.

8) - How's the math homework coming?

- I thought you could shed some light on it.

9) - Why does your sister always have to visit on Sundays?

- I wish you'd quit flogging a dead horse!

10) - Got any money?

- I'm flat broke.

Exercise 2

Students wishing to pursue careers in television broadcasting or journalism may have many things to consider. Today, I'd like to begin by speaking to those of you wanting to be a news anchor person or television celebrity. Well, it's usually best to start out at the local level. Many people who want to break into television do so at the beginning by approaching local networks in their state. From there, your program may be syndicated on a national level if it is successful enough. Here, by "success," I mean that success is measured by the number of viewers watching the program. Now, this advice is equally true for those wishing to do the news, as well as those who want to do talk shows. For example, Oprah Winfrey started out doing a small show at a local network in her state, but her talk show is now known and recognized internationally.

Getting that first break can be very tough, though, and I can't emphasize enough that it is really important to know the right people. Very often, jobs are obtained not because of *what* you know, but because of *who* you know. So networking and personal connections are very important. You might even want to consider starting out by doing a clerical or office job at one of these networks as a way of making those essential first contacts.

Now, on the other hand, if you want to be a serious television journalist, that's a slightly different matter. You may want to study journalism or broadcasting at college since some television networks consider academic training to be a very important prerequisite to obtaining these types of jobs. Of course, a whole host of personality traits will also come into play. You may be traveling to dangerous locations to provide commentary on crisis situations, so you'd better not be a nervous person or someone who is easily frightened. Having a clear speaking voice and pleasant appearance is also helpful. Above all, you should be quick-thinking and ready to respond logically to any challenge.

Unit 3

1) Will you leave during the intermission of the performance?

2) Was there an accident at the intersection?

3) Did the realtor say you could get a good price for your house?

4) Will you quit your job if you don't get a raise?

5) How did you do on the math test?

6) Did the mail carrier come by yet?

7) Can I borrow your eraser for a minute?

8) Have you seen the new movie?

9) How many beers did he drink?

10) Will Janet come with Billy to the party?

Exercise 3

Some people believe that the profession of teaching is fraught with difficulties these days. Of course, it's true that teaching – especially in state high schools – can present challenges even to the most experienced of teachers. Many teachers agree that perhaps the most serious problem is that of disruptive or violent teenagers. These students can make it very difficult to establish a good learning environment. Not only are they exceptionally difficult to teach, but they also can threaten other students or make them feel uncomfortable.

Funding might also be a problem. Since state high schools receive money from the government for their support, the purchase of resources such as books, equipment, and facilities, depends on this financial assistance. If the state or national economy experiences a downturn, this can have a negative effect on the money available to help schools, and some educational institutions may face the agonizing decision of having to discontinue certain classes or programs simply because there isn't enough money available. Because of these and other demands, some teachers have changed careers after deciding that the demands of the educational system and state bureaucracy have made their work too stressful.

However, dedicated teachers agree that teaching can be highly rewarding. Helping students gain new knowledge certainly empowers them and helps them to improve their lives. Teachers to whom I have spoken describe the joy teaching brings them, especially when a student has grasped a difficult concept or idea after a period of struggling or misapprehension. Of course, teachers also receive intellectual stimulation from their work. Many teachers believe that they learn new things themselves as they prepare their lessons and teach their classes.

Unit 4

1)   - Billy has stolen from his mother's purse again!

      - That really takes the cake!

2)   - Will you be going to college this year?

      - I hope to begin in the fall.

3)   - Betty has gotten pretty fat lately.

      - I'll say! She eats potato chips and candy all day long.

4)   - It was a good thing the meeting adjourned early.

      - Yeah, everybody was dying for a smoke.

5)   - Mary Jo asked me for money again.

      - She's got a lot of nerve!

6)   - Will you be getting any money from your grandma's estate?

      - I should be so lucky!

7)   - Is Anna a hard worker?

      - I wouldn't say she is the most industrious person I know.

8)   - Did you tell the professor that you were sick yesterday?

      - Oh, what's the point!

9)   - What will we do if Bob isn't home when we get there?

      - We'll cross that bridge when we come to it.

10)   - John is one of the meanest people I know!

       - You're telling me!

Exercise 4

A group of English separatists known as the Pilgrims first left England to live in Amsterdam in 1608. After spending a few years in their new city, though, many members of the group felt that they did not have enough independence. So, in 1617, the Pilgrims decided to leave Amsterdam to emigrate to America. However, many of these separatists were poor farmers who did not have much education or social status, and, not surprisingly, the group had many financial problems that prevented them from beginning their journey. Although their inability to finance themselves caused many disputes and disagreements, the Pilgrims finally managed to obtain financing from a well-known and affluent London businessman named Thomas Weston.

Having obtained Weston's monetary support, the group returned to England to pick up some additional passengers and boarded a large ship called the *Mayflower* on September 16, 1620. After 65 days at sea, the Pilgrims reached America. Plymouth, a town about 35 miles southeast of Boston in the New England state of Massachusetts, was established by the Pilgrims on December 21, 1620. Even though the early days of their new lives were filled with hope and promise, the harsh winter proved to be too much for some of the settlers. Nearly half of the Pilgrims died during that first winter, but those who lived went on to work hard and prosper.

The Pilgrims also created their own government by writing the Mayflower Compact, a document which is commonly believed to be the first basis of written law in America. This new government had many influential leaders. John Alden, who came to America on the *Mayflower*, signed the Mayflower Compact and held various public offices. William Bradford helped to establish the town of Plymouth and was the governor of the Plymouth Colony for more than 30 years. Miles Standish worked as a political advisor and was also a valued member of the Plymouth community.

Unit 5

1) Could you give me a lift?

2) If I ask the boss for a raise, do you think it will fly?

3) Were you able to find an empty space in the parking lot?

4) Could you empty the wastebasket into the garbage can, please?

5) Have you ever been there before?

6) Did you remember to take your swimming suit to the pool?

7) Will he get in touch with you?

8) Would you please write your last name in the space provided?

9) Did you mow the grass in the front yard yesterday?

10) Want to go downtown tonight?

Exercise 5

There are many excellent reasons to study dramatic arts during your years at college. Indeed, most employers agree that drama classes provide students with skills such as public speaking, in addition to helping build self-confidence, a trait that is very much sought-after in today's job market.

A wide array of classes and workshops in the dramatic arts is available at most colleges and universities. First of all, the student may be required to attend productions at various local and regional theaters. Students are not merely passive members of the audience during these performances. Rather, they are expected to analyze and critique the production, noting what the actors have done well, as well as what they have done poorly.

Students may also be expected to study the history of the theater. These types of courses generally involve a review of dramatic developments of the theaters of the Greek, Roman, Neoclassic, and Elizabethan periods. The student might be expected to become acquainted with dramatic literature of these periods, such as that of the Hellenic Golden Age.

Finally, the student will be expected to perform on stage, of course. This may mean that the student needs to overcome stage fright – the feeling of extreme nervousness that often prevents one from performing well or speaking confidently in front of an audience. The student can even work on a college production to learn the principles of acting for television or film. Such courses usually include an introduction to the mechanics of stage movement, emotional and imaginative responsiveness, the fundamentals of understanding particular characters, and a study of the actor's physical and psychological resources.

Unit 6

1)   - My husband always cooks and cleans for me.

         - Well, that should tell you something!

2)   - Did your son make the varsity team?

         - No, he didn't make the grade.

3)   - Shall we eat at McDonald's or Wendy's tonight?

         - I'll leave that up to you.

4)   - Will we have a history quiz today?

         - Your guess is as good as mine!

5)   - Edith left Al because he was cheating on her.

         - Well, he made his bed, and now he can lie in it!

6)   - Are you still working at the plant?

         - No, I just couldn't handle it anymore.

7)   - How did your appointment go with Bob last night?

         - He stood me up.

8)   - Let's go roller skating.

         - I'm not up to that.

9)   - You're five minutes late!

       - Oh, lighten up!

10)   - How is married life treating you, Tom?

       - My wife is really a hard woman to please.

Exercise 6

The tradition of music in the western world originated in the genre of chanting. Prior to the thirteenth century, chant was the dominant mode of music. Notably, chanting was a monophonic form of music. In other words, it consisted of only one sound or voice that combined various notes in a series.

Polyphonic music appeared in the fifteenth century during the early Renaissance period. In contrast to monophonic music, polyphonic music consists of more than one voice or instrument, combining the notes from the different sources together simultaneously. As polyphony developed, musical traditions began to change, meaning that music began to rely on a greater range of voices, from the very high to the very low.

During the end of the sixteenth century, there was an attempt to return to the tradition of Greek drama. This had a particular influence on the opera. As a result, the opera expanded to include oratorios, which are extended sung musical compositions on a particular subject.

The seventeenth century witnessed the proliferation of musical instruments. Musical compositions and arrangements for keyboard instruments, such as the piano and organ, thrived during this period. Music for the orchestra also began to develop at this time.

The eighteenth century was marked by the development of Baroque music. Stringed instruments, particularly the violin, were predominant throughout this epoch. Since many of the German-born composers studied abroad, Baroque music was regarded to possess a truly international style. Other forms of classical music, especially the symphony, also developed during this century.

Beethoven was truly a remarkable and versatile musician. He contributed to almost every style of music during his era, including piano, strings, and symphonies, and he expanded the form of the symphony to include greater orchestration. For these reasons, the music of Beethoven is commonly regarded as establishing the end of the classical period.

Unit 7

1) Will you take your camper with you on vacation?

2) Why hasn't the server brought our food yet?

3) Didn't the accident happen when he passed on the hill?

4) What kind of whiskey do you prefer?

5) How did Mary and Betty get along with each other?

6) Could I have a bus schedule for the number 12, please?

7) Excuse me, do you have a rest room?

8) Didn't you think that her story was a fib?

9) John is a patrolman. Doesn't he have a lot of pull with the police?

10) Did your co-workers show you the ropes at the office?

Exercise 7

The burglary at the Watergate building in 1972 is one of the most famous crimes ever recorded in America. The break-in took place on June 17 of that year when five men, impeccably dressed in suits and ties, were caught by a security guard after they had surreptitiously entered the office of the headquarters of the Democratic National Committee.

The security guard reported that the burglary was apparently planned. He told the police that a piece of tape had been placed over a lock in a door leading to the headquarters in order to keep the door open. The police also discovered that the men were wearing gloves and that they had filled their pockets with sequentially numbered one-hundred-dollar bills. Most importantly, the men were carrying burglary tools.

Even though a ringleader was not named, the police later confirmed that the men were part of a professional ring. The police reported that nothing was stolen, and it was evident that the men had chosen the offices for their break-in because they were searching for specific documents. It is also known that the men were attempting to repair a bug, which is a secret telephone listening device, that they had installed three weeks before the break-in.

The Watergate burglary had many aspects, but at its center was President Richard Nixon. The lawbreaking reached to various branches of the United States government and included administrators within the White House. It later emerged that the five men who conducted the burglary worked under the direction of G. Gordon Liddy, who was President Nixon's finance counsel. Liddy was in charge of an organization known as CREEP, which stands for the Committee for the Re-election of the President.

Throughout the investigation of the burglary, government officials denied involvement in the crime. An extensive cover-up operation followed in an attempt to conceal those who were involved in planning the break-in. Yet, this subterfuge failed when the FBI investigated the one-hundred-dollar bills that were found in the pockets of the burglars. After making inquiries, the FBI discovered that this money originated from the CREEP organization, thereby confirming governmental involvement. In the end, men who had entered the highest branches of the American government to serve and protect the people went to prison instead.

Unit 8

1)   - Do you want to come with us to the concert?

         - Count me in!

2)   - Bob has quite a sense of humor.

         - I'll say! He really cracks me up!

3)   - Is Mary's dad really strict?

         - Yes. He really makes her toe the line.

4)   - I've been dropped from the varsity team.

         - How come?

5)   - Were they robbed or burglarized?

         - Doesn't it amount to the same thing?

6)   - I heard you flunked another history test.

         - Oh well! That's the way the cookie crumbles!

7)   - Bob has been in business for ten years.

         - Well, he must be doing something right.

8)   - How are things going with your new mother-in-law?

         - Don't even ask!

9)   - Did he say to turn left or right at the corner?

         - I didn't catch it.

10)   - I can't understand what Sandra sees in Tom.

         - Yeah, what a zero!

Exercise 8

The study of the philosophy of human nature is often regarded as an investigation into the meaning of life. This subject usually deals with four key problem areas: human choice, human thought, human personality, and the unity of the human being. A consideration of these four problem areas can also include scientific and artistic viewpoints on the nature of human life.

The first problem area, human choice, asks whether human beings can really make decisions that can change their futures. Conversely, it investigates to what extent the individual's future is fixed and pre-determined by cosmic forces outside the control of human beings. In the second problem area, human thought, epistemology is considered. Epistemology means the study of knowledge; it should not be confused with ontology, the study of being or existence. The third key issue, human personality, emphasizes aspects of human life that are beyond mental processes. It takes a look at emotional, spiritual, and communal elements. Importantly, the study of the communal aspect focuses on community and communication, rather than on government or the philosophy of the state.

Finally, the fourth problem, the unity of the human being, explores the first three areas more fully and asks whether there is any unifying basis for human choice, thought, and personality. In other words, while the human is an inherently complex being, there must be a unity or wholeness underlying these complications. The study of the philosophy of human nature should enable an individual to contemplate more deeply vital human issues, including an engagement with political, cultural, and social debates. Not surprisingly, the works of Plato and Aristotle are generally regarded as the foundation for this subject.

Unit 9

1) Did you park your car parallel to the curb?

2) Aren't fried oysters the specialty of the house?

3) If you haven't been smoking, why is the ashtray full of cigarette butts?

4) Didn't you put the detergent on top of the washer?

5) Haven't you changed a baby's diaper before?

6) Don't you just hate John's negative attitude?

7) Do you feel at ease at Sarah's house?

8) Was the vote at the meeting unanimous?

9) Should the orange juice be diluted?

10) Wasn't there a public outcry about the tax increase?

Exercise 9

Organic farming has become one of the fastest growing trends in agriculture recently. Over the past ten years, sales of organic products in the United States have increased a staggering 20 percent, with retail sales per year of more than nine billion dollars. American farmers have realized that organic farming is an incredibly cost-effective method because it can potentially be used to control costs, as well as to appeal to higher-priced markets.

Apart from these monetary benefits, organic farming also naturally results in positive ecological outcomes for the environment. Organic farming relies on practices that do not harm the environment, and for this reason, chemicals and synthetic medicines are prohibited. All kinds of agricultural products can be produced organically, including grains, meat, eggs, and milk.

In order for agricultural products to be certified as organic, they must be grown and processed according to regulations established by the USDA, the United States Department of Agriculture. Certification involves two stages: the submission of a system plan and an inspection of processing facilities. The certification process is a stringent one and must be undertaken every year.

In spite of these rigorous requirements, some people remain concerned about the safety of organic food. However, research has shown that organic produce contains lower levels of both chemicals and bacteria than food which is produced using conventional farming methods.

Last but not least, organic farms are better for wildlife that those run conventionally. Scientists have discovered that organic farms contain more species of plants, birds, and insects due to the fact that the absence of chemicals from pesticides and fertilizers makes these areas richer habitats for animals.

Unit 10

1) - I can't find my car keys anywhere.

   - Have you really searched high and low?

2) - Did that horror movie on the late show scare you?

   - Yeah, it gave me the creeps.

3) - I couldn't make out what Jason was saying.

   - I know! He talks a mile a minute.

4) - I heard that Tom is working in Indianapolis.

   - Yes, he is a stockbroker there.

5) - Did you have any trouble with your biology final?

   - No, it was a piece of cake.

6) - John thinks that Sue will come back to him after all.

   - Well, I think he'd better wake up and smell the coffee.

7) - Do you go bowling often?

   - Only once in a blue moon.

8) - It was either lie or upset her.

   - Well, I hope you chose the lesser of two evils.

9) - I think we'd better be heading home.

   - Come on!

10) - I've just heard some juicy gossip about Annette.

    - Well, you'd better not cast aspersions on her character.

Exercise 10

Cancer, a group of more than one hundred different types of disease, occurs when cells in the body begin to divide abnormally and continue dividing and forming more cells without control or order. Importantly, all internal organs of the body consist of cells, which normally divide to produce more cells when the body requires them. This is a natural, orderly process that keeps human beings healthy.

However, if a cell divides when it is not necessary, a large growth called a tumor can form. These tumors can usually be removed, and in many cases, they do not come back. Unfortunately, in some cases the cancer from the original tumor spreads. The spread of cancer in this way is called metastasis.

There are some factors which are known to increase the risk of cancer. Smoking is the largest single cause of death from cancer in the United States. One-third of the deaths from cancer each year are related to smoking, making tobacco use the most preventable cause of death in this country.

Choice of food can also be linked to cancer. Research shows that there is a link between high-fat food and certain cancers, and being seriously overweight is also a cancer risk. Cancer risk can therefore be reduced by cutting down on fatty food and eating generous amounts of fruit and vegetables.

Skin cancer is the most common type of cancer for both men and women. Repeated exposure to the sun, through sunbathing for example, greatly increases a person's chance of developing this kind of cancer. As a general rule, it is usually best to avoid the sun during midday and early afternoon, but when this is not possible, one should be sure to use protective sun-blocking creams.

Cancer is now the second leading cause of death in the United States. One-third of all American women and half of all American men will develop some form of cancer during their lifetimes. Yet, millions of people have been successfully treated for cancer. The sooner cancer is found and treatment starts, the better one's chances are for successfully treating the cancer and living a long and healthy life.

Unit 11

1) Will you take care of the kids while I'm away?

2) What did your banker say?

3) Did you hear that their house burned to the ground?

4) Did you apply for that job in the want ad?

5) Do you have something up your sleeve?

6) How do you earn a living?

7) Will she heed your advice?

8) Is it yours for keeps?

9) Do you have faith in Scott's abilities?

10) Would you like another helping?

Exercise 11

Most psychological theories support the view that there are sixteen personality types. These sixteen personalities are based on the combination of four categories of two opposite functions which individuals use in their lives.

The first of these four categories describes the way in which we relate to other people and receive our simulation. The term "extrovert" is used describe people who prefer to interact with the outside world, including interactions with other people. On the other hand, the function "introvert" includes those who prefer to receive simulation from within themselves; that is, they are internally-focused individuals.

The individual's method of receiving information is included in the second category. Here, the opposite functions are "sensing" and "intuitive." "Sensing" individuals function by trusting their five senses. In other words, "sensing" involves perceiving information that is external to the individual. Conversely, the "intuitive" function means that a person relies on instinct, which is his or her inner voice, to process information.

The third category takes a look at how we prefer to make decisions. Those who would rather come to decisions based on objective facts and logic use the "thinking" function. However, those who make choices in life according to their own personal, subjective value systems use the opposite "feeling" function.

The fourth and final category is concerned with how a person deals with or manages day-to-day life. If a person is organized and more comfortable with schedules, timetables, and structure, he or she can be described as "judging." The opposite function is "perceiving." "Perceiving" individuals prefer casual, varied, and open arrangements that allow for flexibility.

As mentioned previously, it is the combination of these four functions that determines which one of the sixteen personality types the individual possesses. For example, one personality type is the introverted-intuitive-feeling-judger. This type of personality prefers to receive information internally, relying on instinct, basing decisions on an internal value system, and managing the outside world according to lists and schedules.

Unit 12

1)   - How is your relationship with Sue going?

       - I told her to take a hike!

2)   - How about going to Cleveland for the weekend?

       - No, I'm afraid it's out of the question.

3)   - It's time to clear up the problem once and for all.

       - I agree whole-heartedly.

4)   - Are college finals really that important?

       - You bet! It can make the difference between passing and failing.

5)   - I'll touch base with you next week.

        - Yes, please give me a call.

6)   - Bob's having an affair with his wife's best friend!

        - Wow! Talk about flirting with disaster!

7)   - Won't you get your hair cut for your date with Sharon?

        - No way! What you see is what you get!

8)   - Have you told Mary what you want for your birthday present?

        - Well, I've dropped a few hints.

9)   - How was your trip to Rio?

        - It was beyond my wildest dreams!

10)   - I told my boss that he was a nitwit.

        - Well, you'd better not cut off your nose to spite your face.

Exercise 12

Meriwether Lewis and William Clark were perhaps the two most famous explorers of the American West. In 1804, the two men began an expedition westward across the area of the United States that was then known as the Louisiana Territory, and along their way, they encountered unknown people and harsh climatic conditions.

Lewis was born on August 18, 1774 in the state of Virginia. Clark was also born in Virginia, although he was four years older than Lewis. The two men met when Lewis joined the local militia, of which Clark was in command. During their experiences in combat, Lewis and Clark made a long-lasting friendship.

United States President Thomas Jefferson had been Lewis's neighbor, and when Lewis was a young captain in the army, he received a letter from Jefferson offering him a job in charge of an expedition to explore the Western country.

On February 28, 1803, the United States Congress finally approved the financing for the expedition. At this time, Lewis told President Jefferson that it would be preferable to have a partner for the rigorous journey westward. With Jefferson's permission, Lewis offered the assignment to his friend Clark.

In terms of their backgrounds, abilities, and interests, Lewis and Clark had a great deal in common. They both possessed many traits that would prove to be crucial for such a daunting expedition: they were intelligent, courageous, and loved adventure, and because of their time in the army, they were calm under pressure and able to make important decisions quickly.

The journey that Lewis and Clark made was more than 8,000 miles in length and lasted for nearly two and a half years. The team charted their course by following the Missouri River, and they were responsible for discovering the Northwest Passage. When their expedition had safely concluded, President Jefferson purchased the Louisiana Territory for fifteen million dollars.

Tragically, Lewis died at the age of 35, only three years after the expedition had finished. Clark lived a long and prosperous life in the state of Missouri, where he died peacefully in 1838. It is commonly believed that both men are worthy of laud and praise, providing later generations with an example of heroic patriotism and nationalistic vision.

Unit 13

Question 1:

Will you be going to college soon?

I hope to begin in the fall.

That's great. Hopefully you'll get a full scholarship.

I should be so lucky!

Question 2:

What are your finances like right now?

I'm flat broke.

Well, I've told you before that you need to try to save a little each month.

I wish you'd quit flogging a dead horse.

Question 3:

You really take me for granted!

Oh, look . . . I'm really sorry. Wow . . . I mean, I was just hoping you'd be more enthusiastic about this. Is that why you asked for your old job back?

Yes, I just couldn't handle it anymore.

Look, I'm glad we spoke about this. I'll discuss your situation with the other managers in the meeting tomorrow.

Question 4:

My wife is really a hard woman to please.

Well, the first few months of marriage can be a bit difficult sometimes.

You're telling me!

Maybe the two of you just need a weekend away to recharge and reconnect.

Question 5:

Did your son make the varsity team?

No, he didn't make the grade.

Oh, what a shame. He's been to every practice and worked so hard. Have you considered speaking to the coach about it?

I'm not up to that.

Question 6:

Hey, Tom. Great to see you. How is your home improvement project coming along?

I thought you could shed some light on it.

Okay, I can give you a hand next time I come over. I'm free this Saturday. Can I touch base with you on Saturday morning before I leave my house?

Yes, please give me a call.

Question 7:

Have you heard anything yet about that new job you interviewed for?

Not yet, but I'll keep you posted.

It sounds like there were a lot of applicants. I know from my own experience that it can be really hard getting work sometimes.

Don't rain on my parade!

Question 8:

I wouldn't say she's the most industrious person I know.

I hate to speak badly about other people, especially Mary . . . she's done an awful lot for me . . . but . . . you know . . . she takes half hour breaks when we're only allowed ten minutes.

She's got a lot of nerve.

You're right. I don't see how she hasn't been fired yet.

Question 9:

Is your friend still eating a lot of junk food?

Yeah, she eats potato chips and candy all day long.

Um . . . To be honest, I'm getting a bit concerned about her health. There are things like diabetes and heart disease to think about at that weight.

Question 10:

Hi John. Are you enjoying the concert?

It's starting to grow on me.

When I started going to these events, I didn't enjoy classical music either. But I have to admit, I do like it now. It's so relaxing.

Question 11:

Have you heard the news? I've heard that they're going to close that bank we use on Main Street. Where are we going to put our money then?

We'll cross that bridge when we come to it.

Well . . . I don't know about that. I mean, we have some advanced warning. Maybe we should start thinking about our other options.

Question 12:

How did your appointment with the manager go yesterday?

He stood me up.

Oh . . . really? Maybe he had another appointment at the last minute or something. The same thing happened to me too about a month ago. He did apologize the next day, though.

Well, that should tell you something.

Question 13:

Have you heard that our classmate is in the county jail?

How come?

Well, he stole a video game from the store and he got caught. Do you think we should go visit him or something?

No, he made his bed and now he can lie in it.

Question 14:

Come on! We need to get going. We're going to be late to the wedding.

Oh, lighten up!

Seriously?! I can't believe your attitude sometimes!

Oh, what's the point!

Question 15:

Did you have any trouble filing the report?

No, it was a piece of cake.

Oh, wow . . . I'll have to give you something more challenging next time.

Unit 14

Question 1:

I had to decide in that moment whether to lie to her or to tell the truth and upset her.

Well, I hope you chose the lesser of two evils.

I hope I did. I ended up telling her a white lie in the end. Do you think it was the right thing to do?

Yeah, I agree whole-heartedly.

Question 2:

How about coming on a road trip with us this weekend?

No, I'm afraid it's out of the question.

Oh, right, you need to study. Is your final exam really that important though?

You bet! It can make the difference between passing and failing.

Question 3:

I just heard that she is cheating on her husband.

Well, you'd better not cast aspersions on her character.

No . . . I know . . . You're totally right. I gossip way too much.

Question 4:

I couldn't make out what the professor was saying.

I know. He talks a mile a minute.

Did he say that the essay is due on Friday?

Don't even ask! I didn't catch it.

Question 5:

Did the movie scare you?

Yeah, it gave me the creeps.

Do you go to scary movies often?

No, only once in a blue moon.

Question 6:

Toby thinks that he will get his job back, even though he insulted the boss.

Well, I think he'd better wake up and smell the coffee.

Yeah, I know. He just seems to be oblivious to the situation. I mean, how out of it can a person be?

Yeah, what a zero.

Question 7:

Amal told me that she can't go to the party. Her dad won't let her. He must be really strict.

Yeah, he really makes her toe the line.

Well, I just can't understand that. I mean, I think that when I'm a parent, I'll let my children make their own decisions when they get older.

Question 8:

I heard your car was completely wrecked in the accident. Are you upset about it?

No, that's the way the cookie crumbles.

You know what? You're right. The important thing is that no one got injured.

Question 9:

I'd really like to get some advice from Carlos. He's been running a successful business now for 25 years, you know.

Well, he must be doing something right.

Absolutely! I hope he has time to talk to me.

Question 10:

I told her to take a hike!

Oh really? Uh . . . I know it's none of my business, but maybe you should try being a little bit nicer to her.

No way! What you see is what you get!

Well, I guess you have to know what you're comfortable with.

Question 11:

Do you want to come with us?

Yeah, count me in.

Great, let's finish our homework, then do the dishes, and then we can take off.

Question 12:

I can't find my jacket anywhere.

Have you really searched high and low?

Uh . . . How frustrating . . . I just don't understand why you question me over little things like this sometimes!

Wow! What's come over you?

Question 13:

Well, what did you make of that exam?

Can I be frank?

Yeah, of course. That's why I asked. So do you think you passed?

No, and I'm just beside myself.

Question 14:

She wore that dress to the party with the tags hidden, then she returned it to the shop the next day to get her money back.

That really takes the cake!

Yeah, I know. And it's not the first time she's done it either. She's going to get caught one of these times.

Question 15:

If you keep coming in late to work like this, there are going to be consequences.

I see where you're going with this.

Yeah, that's right. Consider this your last warning.

That's good to know.

Unit 15

SPEAKER 1: Today, we're going to talk about good nutrition. Now, everybody knows that good nutrition is essential for good health. Indeed, a healthy diet can help a person to maintain a good body weight, promote mental wellbeing, and even reduce the risk of disease. So, first of all today, we are going to look at the answer to the question: What does healthy nutrition consist of?

SPEAKER 2: Well . . . first of all, a healthy diet must include food from four major groups. These four groups are carbohydrate, fruit, vegetables, and protein. The first of the four groups, carbohydrate, includes food like potatoes, bread, and cereals, and is essential for providing a person with energy.

SPEAKER 1: Although carbohydrates seem to have gotten bad press lately, in fact, they are an essential part of healthy nutrition, because . . . well . . . importantly, they provide the building blocks for supplying energy to the body.

The second and third food groups are fruit and vegetables – although some people would just include these as one group. This may seem easy to understand at first blush, but it is worth pointing out that good nutrition depends on eating a variety of fruit and vegetables. While the old adage "An apple a day keeps the doctor away" may appear to be sound advice, eating the same fruit or vegetables daily . . . um. . . it's not the best advice in reality. The amount of fruit and vegetables . . . now that's also important to bear in mind. Most medical practitioners in the United States now recommend a minimum consumption of five portions of fruit or vegetables every day.

SPEAKER 2: Protein includes food such as meat and fish, as well as dairy products, like milk and cheese. However, lean protein is better than fatty protein, so be sure to limit the amount of red meat, rich cheeses, and cream that you eat. In addition to limiting your fat intake, you should also be careful about the amount of sugar that you eat.

SPEAKER 1: Next, let's move on and look at the health risks posed by processed or convenience food. Of course, fresh food is far better than processed food. Packaged food often contains chemicals, such as additives to enhance the color of the food or preservatives that give the food a longer life.

SPEAKER 2: These chemicals are not good for the health for two reasons. First of all, they are not natural and may perhaps be linked to disease in the long term. In addition, they may block the body's ability to absorb energy and nutrients from food, with nutrients being the essential vitamins and minerals that are required for healthy bodily function.

UNIT 16

SPEAKER 1: This afternoon, we'll be looking at the function of the human brain. We will also be talking about the way the function, as well as the dysfunction, of the human brain is measured. Now as you may know, it was in 1929 that electrical activity in the human brain was first discovered. Hans Berger, the German psychiatrist who made the discovery, was despondent to find out, though, that his research was quickly dismissed by many other scientists.

The work of Berger was confirmed three years later in 1932 when Edgar Adrian, a Briton, clearly demonstrated that the brain, like the heart, is profuse in its electrical activity. Because of Adrian's work, we know that the electrical impulses in the brain, called brain waves, are a mixture of four different frequencies. Here, I should say first of all that by "frequency" we are referring to the number of electrical impulses that occur in the brain per second.

So, as I was saying, there are four types of brain waves. Alpha waves occur in a state of relaxation, while beta waves occur when a person is alert. In addition, delta waves take place during sleep, but they can also occur dysfunctionally when the brain has been severely damaged. Finally, theta waves are of a frequency that is somewhere in between alpha and delta. It seems that the purpose of theta waves is solely to facilitate the combination of the other brain waves.

The whole notion of brain waves, then, feeds into the current controversy about death, especially brain death. Of course, this is considered to be very rudimentary, but yet is a very essential question, not only in medicine, but also in law and religion. Some people believe that brain death is characterized by the failure of the cerebral cortex to function. Now, you'll remember that the cerebral cortex is the thinking part of the brain, so under this viewpoint, if a person is no longer physically capable of rational thought, they are considered "brain dead." On the other hand, some say that mere damage to the cerebral cortex is not enough. They assert that the brain stem function must also cease before a person can be declared dead, because the cerebral cortex is responsible for other bodily processes.

So, for these myriad reasons, it has become very important to measure brain activity. Now . . . in order to measure brain activity and function, there are various types of equipment, which can perform various types of tests. For instance, we have traditionally used CAT and PET scans for this purpose.

SPEAKER 2: The PET scan works by means of an inert radioactive substance given to a patient, and this allows the doctor to observe the movement of the substance through the brain. As far as the CAT scan, well . . . they are like an X-ray of the brain, which is then displayed on a computer screen. The PET scan shows up as one image, and that image will have different colors. And each one of the colors displays the pattern of the brain activity. With the CAT scan . . .

that's a cross-section, so unlike the PET scan, it can be viewed from different angles or positions. And of course, as far as patients are concerned, the CAT is far less invasive because they don't need to ingest a radioactive substance.

SPEAKER 1: In addition to CAT and PET scans, we now have an MRI scan, which as you know works according to the principles of magnetism. The MRI is perhaps the most indispensable of all of the various scans due to its ability to map the brain in three dimensions.

UNIT 17

SPEAKER 1: Good afternoon, everyone. Today, we're going to be discussing educational strategies. So, let's look at the student readiness model. What do we mean by the student readiness model? Well, teachers quickly realize that students are individuals, each operating at different levels of ability. For some students, this might mean that they are operating above the average ability level of their contemporaries, while for others . . . um . . . they may be functioning at a level that is below average. Then, too, there are the students who are in what can be called a "comfort zone." These students are learning at the optimum learning level: they are being challenged and learning new things, but yet they don't feel overwhelmed or inundated by the new information.

Okay . . . just to complicate things, we also have to remember that student readiness is not a static entity. In other words, it is constantly changing. Some students will become more confident throughout the semester and will be able to increase their "student readiness." And, unfortunately, other students may fall behind and might slip to a below-average position.

Therefore, the onus falls on teachers not only to work out how best to design the curriculum, but also how to structure classroom learning activities that are going to challenge the maximum number of students. The strategy of "question adjustment" can be deployed to help bridge the gap between those students with low readiness and those with high readiness.

SPEAKER 2: "Question adjustment" means that the teacher will ask questions at a variety of different levels of difficulty. There will be some so-called "easy" questions to build the confidence of the students who are less ready. And then, there will also be some really difficult questions, which are supposed to stretch the more capable students, who are the most ready.

SPEAKER 1: Let's move on to the area of formal assessment, in other words, quizzes and tests and so on.

SPEAKER 2: The formal ones are those that count towards the mark or grade for the course. But the informal ones don't.

SPEAKER 1: The purpose of giving the informal assessment is to help build student confidence. Readiness begets confidence, but conversely, confidence can also help to improve a student's level of readiness.

UNIT 18

SPEAKER 1: We're going to talk about a worrying sociological problem, that of teenage smoking. Although the trends show that smoking by adults has been declining steadily over the past few decades, the percentage of teenagers who smoke only started to drop in the late 1990s. In fact, the current statistics on this are really quite alarming because at present the rate of teenagers who smoke is nearly fifty greater than the rate for adult smokers.

SPEAKER 2: Teenagers are more prone to pressure from their friends – peer pressure – and so of course they want to fit in with their social group and smoking is one way to do that. The increase in the use of things like the internet . . . and with a lot of parents working long hours, kids feel a bit alienated: he's just going to feel alone and not connected to anybody else but his friends and then of course he's more susceptible to fall into the trap of smoking because of peer pressure.

SPEAKER 1: But, you know, peer pressure has always existed from time immemorial. In fact, recent research shows that the rise in teenage smoking in the 1990s primarily took place in the youth from more affluent families – you know, their parents were working and earning good incomes, so of course the children were not from disadvantaged homes as some sociologists would like us to believe . . . quite the opposite . . . the most striking and precipitous rise was in teenagers with the most financially advantageous backgrounds.

And we know that because of various law suits against the major tobacco companies, the price of cigarettes actually declined sharply in the 1990s, which of course added fuel to the fire that was already burning in this area socially. What I mean is, paradoxically, these teenagers were from well-off families and could have afforded to pay the higher prices, yet contrary to these market forces, the price of tobacco products was reduced during this time.

Okay . . . so from this we can surmise that price doesn't really appear to be a factor in smoking by teens. Probably, this is because teenagers often view themselves as "experimental smokers."

SPEAKER 2: They see their own smoking behavior as an experiment. So, what that implies is that these kids think they are just trying it out, so they aren't necessarily going to do it – I mean smoke – for their lifetimes. They just view it as something they can try and then stop later. Quitting smoking is an extremely difficult thing to do. It can even be tougher than beating drug addiction because the nicotine in cigarettes is very highly addictive itself.

SPEAKER 1: A recent study on high school students showed that fifty-six percent of the students who smoked predicted that they would not still be smokers five years after graduation. But when the data was gathered five years later, only thirty-one percent of them had actually quit smoking.

ANSWER KEY

UNIT 1

LISTENING

1) B

2) A

3) C

4) A

5) A

6) B

7) A

8) A

9) C

10) B

Exercise 1

1) C

2) B

3) C

4) A

5) C

UNIT 2

LISTENING

1) A
2) B
3) C
4) B
5) C
6) C
7) C
8) A
9) B
10) A

Exercise 2

1) A
2) C
3) B
4) A
5) C

UNIT 3

LISTENING

1) B

2) A

3) A

4) C

5) B

6) A

7) C

8) C

9) B

10) A

Exercise 3

1) C

2) B

3) C

4) B

5) C

UNIT 4

LISTENING

1) C

2) A

3) B

4) C

5) A

6) B

7) C

8) C

9) C

10) B

Exercise 4

1) A

2) C

3) C

4) B

5) C

UNIT 5

LISTENING

1) B

2) A

3) A

4) A

5) B

6) C

7) A

8) B

9) C

10) C

Exercise 5

1) A

2) C

3) C

4) B

5) A

UNIT 6

LISTENING

1) B

2) A

3) A

4) C

5) B

6) A

7) C

8) B

9) A

10) C

Exercise 6

1) A

2) B

3) B

4) C

5) C

UNIT 7

LISTENING

1) A

2) B

3) A

4) B

5) A

6) C

7) C

8) A

9) B

10) C

Exercise 7

1) B

2) C

3) A

4) A

5) B

UNIT 8

LISTENING

1) A

2) A

3) B

4) C

5) A

6) B

7) B

8) A

9) C

10) C

Exercise 8

1) A

2) B

3) C

4) A

5) B

UNIT 9

LISTENING

1) B

2) C

3) A

4) A

5) B

6) B

7) C

8) A

9) B

10) B

Exercise 9

1) B

2) A

3) C

4) B

5) A

UNIT 10

LISTENING

1) A

2) B

3) B

4) A

5) C

6) B

7) C

8) C

9) A

10) A

Exercise 10

1) C

2) C

3) B

4) B

5) B

UNIT 11

LISTENING

1) A
2) C
3) B
4) B
5) A
6) C
7) A
8) B
9) A
10) A

Exercise 11

1) C
2) A
3) B
4) A
5) B

UNIT 12

LISTENING

1) C

2) A

3) A

4) A

5) B

6) C

7) C

8) A

9) C

10) C

Exercise 12

1) C

2) A

3) A

4) C

5) B

UNIT 13

1. C
2. A
3. B
4. C
5. C
6. A
7. B
8. A.
9. A
10. C
11. B
12. C
13. B
14. B
15. C

UNIT 14

1. C
2. C
3. A
4. A
5. C

6. C

7. A

8. B

9. A

10. B

11. C

12. B

13. C

14. B

15. B

UNIT 15

1) A

2) B

3) C

4) A

5) C

UNIT 16

1) A

2) A

3) B

4) B

5) C

UNIT 17

1) C

2) C

3) A

4) B

5) A

UNIT 18

1) B

2) B

3) C

4) A

5) B